Copyright © 2024 by Brian Ernest Hayward and Published by Brian Hayward for Hayward House Publishing Published by Hayward House and Big Book Box A Member of the Brian Hayward Group All rights reserved. No part of this publication may be reproduced, stored in a retrieval system, or transmitted, in any form or by any means, electronic, mechanical, photocopying, recording, or otherwise, without the prior written permission of the publisher. For information and inquiries , address Hayward House publishing and Hayward Press, Savannah, Ga 31405, Library of Congress Cataloging-in-Publication Data. Hayward, Brian. TITLE=In Jesus Mighty Name Series, Journal WRITING for success in your life / Brian Hayward. p. cm.

PAPERBACK EDITION

ISBN: 9798333968197

Imprint:

Independently published

Self-control. 2. Self-management (Psychology) 3. Success. 4. Success in business. 31405, or visit us at https://www.amazon.com/Brian-Ernest-Hayward/e/B06XT464NM

PRAYER FOR MYSELF AND MY READERS

I was taught by my teacher, Pastor Bill Winston, this prayer. This prayer has served me well, and in due time it will serve you well. Father I come before you in Jesus name, thank you for the anointing that's on me and these lips of clay. I know that because of your blessing, I speak this word today with excellency, accuracy, and boldness. I thank you for thinking through my mind and speaking through my lips and this word will come forth unhindered, and unchecked by any outside force. Now I give you the praise for it and I fully expect signs, wonders, and miracles to confirm your word preached in Jesus name,

AUTHOR BIOGRAPHY

Brian Ernest Hayward is a passionate Author and Inspirational Speaker, internationally known for his unwavering dedication to creating positive change through the power of words. From religious and success books, to adult coloring books and artist BUSINESS, HOW-TO BOOKS, his writings touch on over 400 different subjects. Today, all of Brian's publications are sold worldwide across multiple formats (Paperback, Kindle, and Large Print) and are translated into 21 different languages. He has also participated in over 100 speaking engagements spanning over 38 states.

Table Of Contents

Introduction	7
Chapter 1: Hustle 101 – The School of Hard Knocks	15
Chapter 2: Get Your Hustle Muscle Ready!	21
Chapter 3: The A+ Game Plan	29
Chapter 4: Market Your Marquee Moves	37
Chapter 5: Network, Homework, and Net Worth	48
Chapter 6: Sales Savvy – Close the Deal, Don't Lose the Feel	57
Chapter 7: Balancing the Books – Budgeting for the Hustle	64
Chapter 8: Juggling Jobs and Jazz Hands	72
Chapter 9: Creative Crunch Time – Think Outside the Textbook	79

Chapter 10: The Extra Credit – Going Above and Beyond … 86

Chapter 11: Recess and Recharge – Self-Care for the Hustler … 93

Chapter 12: Graduation Day – Celebrate Your Success … 100

Chapter 13: Hustle and Flow – The Rhythm of Success … 107

Chapter 14: Hustle University – Lifelong Learning … 113

Chapter 15: Epilogue: The Dance Continues … 120

Conclusion: Dance Your Way to Success … 126

Bibliography … 145

NOTES … 146

"Hustle! An Old Business Procedure, not a Dance Move"

Introduction

Welcome to "Hustle! An Old Business Procedure, not a Dance Move" - a humorous yet comprehensive guide to mastering the age-old art of hustling in the  business world. If you think hustling is just a funky dance move, think again! In this book, we're diving deep into the world of assertive, proactive business actions that can lead to supreme success and substantial profits.

Imagine you're back in school, but this time, it's the School of Hard Knocks, where the lessons are tough, the teachers are life experiences, and the diploma is a thriving business and a fat bank account. We're here to make this journey educational and entertaining, with plenty of puns, playful wordplay, and real-life examples to keep you engaged.

In the prologue, we'll set the stage by introducing hustling as a business strategy. You'll get a sneak peek into its history and why it stays a powerful approach in today's competitive market. We'll also outline the book's structure, precisely describing what to expect.

Chapter 1, "Hustle 101 - The School of Hard Knocks," will lay the foundation by explaining the basics of the hustle mindset. You'll learn about the essential qualities of a successful hustler, such as resilience, perseverance, and a never-give-up attitude. We'll also share inspiring stories of famous hustlers who started from scratch and built empires.

In Chapter 2, "Get Your Hustle Muscle Ready!" we'll focus on preparing yourself mentally and physically for the hustle. Business success requires a strong mind and body, so we'll provide tips on developing resilience, staying motivated, and building a solid foundation for your hustle journey.

"The A+ Game Plan" in Chapter 3 will guide you through crafting a winning business strategy. From setting SMART goals to mastering time management, this chapter will equip you with the tools to create a roadmap to success. You'll learn to plan effectively and stay on track to achieve your dreams.

Chapter 4, "Market Your Marquee Moves," will delve into marketing. A hustler needs to be a master marketer. We'll cover strategies for branding yourself and your business, using social media, and making the most of digital platforms to reach your audience.

Networking is a crucial part of hustling, and Chapter 5, "Network, Homework, and Net Worth," will show you how to build and keep valuable connections. We'll teach you how to turn contacts into contracts and grow your net worth through effective networking.

In Chapter 6, "Sales Savvy – Close the Deal, Don't Lose the Feel," you'll master the art of selling. We'll provide techniques for closing deals effectively while keeping authenticity and rapport with your clients. Sales is the lifeblood of any business, and this chapter will ensure you're equipped to seal the deal every time.

Chapter 7, "Balancing the Books — Budgeting for the Hustle," will cover financial literacy. Managing your finances is crucial to sustaining your hustle, so we'll teach you how to budget, save, and invest wisely. You'll learn to manage your cash flow and expenses like a pro.

Chapter 8, "Juggling Jobs and Jazz Hands," is about multitasking and prioritizing tasks. We'll show you how to stay organized amidst the chaos, avoid burnout, and keep a healthy work-life balance.

"Creative Crunch Time – Think Outside the Textbook" in Chapter 9 will encourage you to embrace creativity in your business. Innovative problem-solving techniques and case studies of creative hustling will inspire you to think outside the box and find unique solutions.

Chapter 10, "The Extra Credit – Going Above and Beyond," emphasizes the extra mile importance of exceptional hustlers who exceed expectations and will motivate you to strive for excellence in everything you do.

Chapter 11, "Recess and Recharge – Self-Care for the Hustler," focuses on the importance of self-care. Hustling can be demanding, so we'll provide techniques for stress management and finding joy and fulfillment in your journey.

"Graduation Day – Celebrate Your Success" in Chapter 12 will be a time for reflection and celebration. You'll learn to recognize and celebrate your achievements and plan for future growth and success.

In Chapter 13, "Hustle and Flow – The Rhythm of Success," we'll discuss keeping momentum in the long run. This chapter will address critical themes in adapting to changes and challenges and keeping the hustle alive.

Chapter 14, "Hustle University – Lifelong Learning," will emphasize the importance of continuous improvement. We'll provide resources for ongoing education and skill development to stay ahead in the ever-evolving business world.

Finally, in the epilogue, "The Dance Continues," we'll give final thoughts and encouragement. The hustle is a lifelong journey, and we'll invite you to embrace it fully and share your hustle stories with us.

So, let's get ready to hustle, not just for making money but for the joy of achieving success and making a difference. Welcome to "Hustle! An Old Business Procedure, not a Dance Move"—your ultimate guide to mastering the art of the hustle.

Chapter 1: Hustle 101 – The School of Hard Knocks

Welcome to Hustle 101. In this chapter, we'll explore the  fundamental principles of the hustle mindset. The School of Hard Knocks is where severance is a valuable tourist textbook that sets the stage for your journey. It defines what it means to hustle in the business world and why it's a timeless strategy.

At its core, hustling is about taking proactive, assertive actions to achieve your goals. It's not just about working hard but working smart. This mindset involves constant learning, adapting, and pushing beyond your comfort zone to seize opportunities.

The journey of a hustler is fraught with challenges and setbacks. Resilience is your ability to bounce back from failures, while perseverance is your commitment to keep moving forward despite obstacles. These qualities are crucial for sustaining long-term success.

A successful hustler is self-motivated and driven by a deep sense of purpose. This inner drive propels you forward even when external rewards are not at once visible. Finding and nurturing this drive is essential for keeping momentum.

In the School of Hard Knocks, failures are not endpoints but learning opportunities. Each setback offers valuable lessons that can guide your future actions. Embracing failure as part of the process helps you develop a growth mindset.

We'll delve into the stories of iconic hustlers like Steve Jobs, Oprah Winfrey, and Elon Musk. These individuals started from humble beginnings and faced many challenges, yet their hustle and determination led them to extraordinary success.

Grit is the passion and perseverance for long-term and meaningful goals. It's the ability to persist in something you feel passionate about and persevere when you face obstacles. Hustlers understand that grit is not just a fleeting burst of energy and a sustained effort over time.

Hustling requires a clear vision. This means knowing what you want and having a plan to achieve it. Vision provides direction and purpose, guiding your actions and decisions. Without a clear vision, hustle can become aimless and ineffective.

Networking is a critical part of hustling. Building and nurturing relationships can open doors to new opportunities, resources, and support. Effective networking involves making connections and providing value to others, creating a mutually beneficial dynamic.

Adaptability is another key trait of successful hustlers. The business world is constantly changing, and those who can pivot and adapt to new circumstances are more likely to thrive. Adaptability means staying open to new ideas, embracing change, and continuously learning.

Time management is crucial for keeping productivity and achieving your goals. Hustlers must be masters of their time, effectively balancing various tasks and responsibilities. Prioritizing tasks, setting deadlines, and avoiding procrastination are essential skills in the hustle arsenal.

Self-discipline is about having the control to stick to your plans and follow through on your commitments. It involves making sacrifices and resisting temptations that can derail your progress. Self-discipline is the backbone of consistency, which is vital for long-term success.

Effective communication is a must for hustlers. This includes conveying your ideas and listening actively to others. Good communication builds trust, fosters collaboration, and helps you navigate the complexities of business relationships.

Confidence is a vital attribute for any hustler. Believing in yourself and your abilities can help you overcome self-doubt and take bold actions. Confidence is built through preparation, practice, and the willingness to step out of your comfort zone.

Lastly, a positive attitude can significantly affect your hustle journey. Optimism helps you stay motivated and focused in the face of adversity. A positive mindset attracts opportunities and inspires those around you, creating a supportive environment for your hustle.

Chapter 2: Get Your Hustle Muscle Ready!

Preparing yourself mentally and physically for the hustle is crucial for sustained success. This chapter will delve into the strategies and practices that help build resilience, keep motivation, and lay a solid foundation for your hustle journey.

Mental preparation begins with cultivating a strong mindset. This involves developing a positive outlook, embracing challenges as opportunities for growth, and fostering a relentless determination to succeed. Your mindset is the driving force behind your actions, so it keeps you focused and resilient.

Do essential energy levels fit  and physically fit forty energy levels? Regular exercise, a balanced diet, and sufficient rest can enhance your physical well-being, enabling you to perform at your best. A healthy body supports a healthy mind, creating a synergy that fuels your hustle.

Setting clear and achievable goals is a cornerstone of effective hustling. Goals provide direction and motivation, helping you focus on what matters most. Break your long-term goals into smaller, manageable tasks, and celebrate your progress.

Building a strong support system is another critical aspect of preparing for the hustle. Surround yourself with positive, like-minded individuals who can offer encouragement, advice, and constructive feedback. A supportive network can provide the emotional and practical support you need to keep pushing forward.

Time management is a skill that every hustler must master. Organize your day by prioritizing tasks, setting deadlines, and avoiding distractions. Use planners, calendars, and time-tracking apps to stay on schedule and ensure you're making the most of every moment.

Developing a routine can help set up consistency and discipline in your hustle. Create includes exercise, relaxation, and personal growth. A well-structured routine enables you to stay organized and support a balanced lifestyle.

Continuous learning is vital for staying ahead in the hustle game. Invest in your education by reading books, attending workshops, and seeking out mentors. Stay curious and open to new ideas, and always be on the lookout for opportunities to expand your knowledge and skills.

Stress management is crucial for keeping your well-being and productivity. Practice mindfulness, meditation, or other relaxation techniques to manage stress and stay focused. Taking regular breaks and allowing yourself time to recharge can prevent burnout and keep you energized.

Self-motivation is about finding and nurturing your inner drive. Find what inspires and motivates you and use it as fuel to keep going. Whether it's a personal passion, a financial goal, or the desire to make a difference, tap into that source of motivation to stay committed to your hustle.

Building resilience involves developing the ability to bounce back from setbacks. View challenges as learning opportunities and stay persistent in the face of adversity. Resilience allows you to support a positive attitude and keep moving forward, no matter the obstacles.

Accountability can significantly affect your progress. Set up systems to hold yourself accountable through regular check-ins with a mentor, tracking your goals, or sharing your progress with a trusted friend. Accountability helps you stay on track and keep your momentum.

Self-discipline is the foundation of any successful hustle. Develop the habit of sticking to your plans and following through on your commitments. This involves making sacrifices, resisting temptations, and staying focused on your goals, even when it's challenging.

Visualization is a powerful tool for achieving your goals. Spend time each day visualizing your success and the steps you need to take to get there. This practice can boost your confidence, enhance your focus, and create a mental blueprint for your hustle journey.

Gratitude can enhance your overall well-being and motivation. Take time each day to reflect on what you are thankful for and acknowledge your achievements, no matter how small. A thankful mindset can shift your focus to your hustle's positive aspects and inspire you.

Lastly, keep a growth mindset by embracing challenges and learning from your experiences. Understand that growth and success are processes and be patient with yourself as you navigate the ups and downs of the hustle. A growth mindset encourages continuous improvement and resilience.

Chapter 3: The A+ Game Plan

Creating a winning business strategy is essential for successful hustling. This chapter will guide you through setting SMART goals, mastering time management, and developing a comprehensive plan to achieve your aims.

SMART goals are specific, measurable, achievable, relevant, and time-bound.  Setting SMART goals provides clarity and direction, ensuring your effort is focused and productive. Define your goals clearly, break them, and set deadlines to track your progress.

Effective time management is crucial for maximizing productivity. Prioritize your tasks based on their importance and urgency and distribute your time accordingly. Use techniques like the Pomodoro Technique or time blocking to stay focused and keep daily momentum.

Creating a business plan involves outlining your vision, mission, and aims. A well-crafted business plan serves as a roadmap, guiding your actions and decisions. To create a comprehensive plan, include details on your target market, competitive analysis, marketing strategies, and financial projections.

Market research is essential for understanding your industry and finding opportunities. Conduct thorough research to gather data on market trends, customer preferences, and competitor strategies. Use this information to make informed decisions and refine your business plan.

Finding your target audience is a critical step in developing your game plan. Understand who your customers are, what they need, and how to meet them. Create customer personas to visualize your target audience and tailor your marketing efforts accordingly.

Crafting a unique value proposition sets you apart from competitors. Clearly articulate what makes your product or service unique and why customers should choose you. Your value proposition should address the needs and desires of your target audience, providing a compelling reason to buy from you.

Building a solid brand identity is crucial for setting up credibility and trust. Develop a brand that reflects your values, mission, and vision. Consistent branding across all channels, from your logo and website to your social media profiles, helps create a cohesive and recognizable image.

Marketing strategies are essential for reaching and engaging your audience. Develop a comprehensive marketing plan that includes both online and offline tactics. Utilize social media, content marketing, email campaigns, and other channels to promote your brand and attract customers.

Sales strategies are equally crucial for converting leads into customers. Develop a sales process that guides prospects through the buyer's journey, from first contact to closing the deal. Train your sales team on practical techniques, such as active listening, building rapport, and addressing objections.

Customer Relationship management (CRM) systems can help you manage and nurture customer relationships. Use CRM tools to track interactions, manage leads, and automate follow-ups. Building solid relationships with customers fosters loyalty and encourages repeat business.

Financial planning is a critical aspect of your game plan. Create a budget that outlines your projected income and expenses. Monitor your financial performance regularly and adjust your plan to stay on the strategy. Sound financial management is vital to sustaining your hustle.

Risk management involves finding potential risks and developing strategies to mitigate them. Conduct a risk assessment to find threats to your business, such as market fluctuations, operational challenges, or legal issues. Develop contingency plans to address these risks and ensure business continuity.

Performance metrics help you track your progress and measure success. Name key performance indicators (KPIs) that align with your goals, such as sales revenue, customer acquisition cost, or website traffic. Regularly review your metrics and use the data to make informed decisions.

Continuous improvement is essential for long-term success. Regularly evaluate your game plan, name areas for improvement, and adjust as needed. Stay open to feedback and be willing to adapt your strategies based on new information and changing circumstances.

Celebrating milestones and achievements can boost morale and motivation. Recognize and reward your accomplishments, no matter how small. Celebrating your progress keeps you motivated; by now, you've come on your hustle journey.

Chapter 4: Market Your Marquee Moves

Marketing is the lifeblood of any hustle. This chapter will delve into the strategies and techniques for effectively marketing yourself and your business, building a strong brand, and attracting and keeping customers.

Understanding your market is the first step in developing an effective marketing strategy. Conduct market research to gather insights into your industry, competitors, and target audience. This information will inform your marketing decisions and help you name growth opportunities.

Building a solid brand identity is essential for creating a memorable and trustworthy image. Your brand should reflect your values, mission, and vision and resonate with your target audience. Consistent branding across all channels, from your logo and website to your social media profiles, helps create a cohesive and recognizable image.

Developing a unique value proposition sets you apart from competitors. Clearly articulate what makes your product or service unique and why customers should choose you. Your value proposition should address the needs and desires of your target audience, providing a compelling reason to buy from you.

Content marketing is a powerful tool for engaging and educating your audience. Create valuable and relevant content that addresses the needs and interests of your target audience. Blog posts, videos, podcasts, and social media updates are all effective ways to share your ability and build trust with your audience.

Social media marketing is essential for reaching a broad audience and building a community around your brand. Choose the most popular platforms with your target audience and create a consistent posting schedule. Engage with your followers by responding to comments, sharing user-generated content, and running promotions and contests.

Email marketing is an effective way to nurture leads and keep customer relationships. Build an email list by offering valuable content or incentives, and create regular newsletters that provide updates, promotions, and helpful information. Personalized and targeted emails can increase engagement and conversions.

Search engine optimization (SEO) is crucial for improving online visibility and attracting organic traffic to your website. Perfect your website and content for relevant keywords, ensure your site is mobile-friendly and fast-loading, and regularly update your content and build backlinks to improve your search engine rankings.

Paid advertising can help you reach a larger audience and drive traffic to your website. Use platforms like Google Ads, Facebook Ads, and Instagram Ads to create targeted campaigns that reach your ideal customers. Monitor and analyze your ad performance to perfect your campaigns and maximize your return on investment.

Influencer marketing uses the reach and credibility of  influencers to promote your brand. Find influencers who align with your brand values and have a following that matches your target audience. Collaborate with them on campaigns, product reviews, or sponsored content to increase your brand visibility and credibility.

Public relations (PR) can help you build a positive image and gain media coverage. Develop relationships with journalists and bloggers and create press releases and media kits to share your news and updates. PR can help you reach a wider audience and build trust with potential customers.

Customer reviews and testimonials are powerful tools for building credibility and trust. Encourage satisfied customers to leave reviews on platforms like Google, Yelp, and social media. Display testimonials on your website and marketing materials to showcase your happy customers and their positive experiences.

Networking is an essential part of marketing your business. Attend industry events, join professional organizations, and take part in online communities to connect with potential customers, partners, and influencers. Building relationships through networking can open doors to new opportunities and collaborations.

 Referral programs can help you buy new customers through word-of-mouth marketing. Create a referral program that incentivizes your existing customers to refer their friends and family to your business. Offer rewards like discounts, freebies, or exclusive access to encourage participation.

Measuring the effectiveness of your marketing efforts is crucial for continuous improvement. Use  analytics tools to track key performance metrics like website traffic, conversion rates, and social media engagement. Regularly review your data and adjust your strategies based on your findings.

Innovation and creativity are needed to stand out in a crowded market. Experiment with new marketing techniques and stay opening unconventional approaches. Innovation can help you capture attention, differentiate your brand, and create memorable experiences for your audience.

Chapter 5: Network, Homework, and Net Worth

Networking is a crucial part of the hustle. In this chapter, we'll explore the importance of building  and keeping valuable connections, turning contacts into contracts, and using your network to grow your business and increase your net worth.

Effective networking starts with a clear understanding of your goals and aims. Know what you want to achieve and find connections to help you reach those goals. Whether you're looking for mentors, partners, clients, or investors, having a clear focus will guide your networking efforts.

Building genuine relationships is vital to successful networking. Approach networking with a mindset of giving rather than just taking. Offer value to others by  sharing your knowledge, aiding, and making introductions. Genuine relationships are built on trust and mutual respect.

Attending industry events, conferences, and trade shows is an excellent way to meet potential connections. These events provide opportunities to learn from experts, stay updated on industry trends, and network with like-minded professionals. Be prepared with a clear elevator pitch and business cards to make a lasting impression.

Joining professional organizations and online communities can expand your network and provide valuable resources. Participate actively in discussions, share your insights, and offer help to others. Being an active and contributing member can increase your visibility and credibility within the community.

Social media platforms like LinkedIn, Twitter, and Facebook can help you connect with professionals in your industry. Share valuable content, engage with others, and  take part in online discussions to build your presence. Social media can be a powerful tool for expanding your network and reaching a wider audience.

Following up with new connections is essential for building and keeping relationships. After meeting someone at an event or online, send a personalized follow-up message to express your appreciation and reinforce the connection. Regularly check in with contacts to remember and show how genuine interest.

Leveraging your existing network can open doors to new opportunities. Ask for introductions, referrals, and recommendations from your contacts. A warm introduction from a trusted connection can be more effective than a cold outreach, increasing your chances of success.

Providing value to your network is crucial for keeping strong relationships. Share your ability, offer help, and support others in their endeavors. Being known as a valuable and reliable resource can strengthen your reputation and encourage others to reciprocate.

Building a personal brand can enhance your networking efforts. Your personal brand is the unique  combination of skills, experiences, and values that make you stand out. Consistently communicate your brand through your online presence, interactions, and content to attract like-minded professionals.

Developing practical communication skills is essential for networking. Practice active listening, ask thoughtful questions, and show genuine interest in others. Effective communication builds rapport, fosters trust, and helps you understand your connections' needs and goals.

Participating in networking groups and masterminds can provide ongoing support and accountability. These groups offer a platform to share ideas, seek advice, and collaborate with others. Being part of a supportive network can boost your confidence and help you stay motivated.

Turning contacts into contracts involves naming opportunities for collaboration and business deals. Look for ways to align your goals and interests with your connections. Propose mutually beneficial partnerships and clearly communicate your value to the team. A reputation as a reliable and trustworthy professional can enhance your networking success. Deliver on your promises, keep integrity, and treat others with respect. A strong reputation can attract more opportunities and encourage others to refer you to their network.

Networking is an ongoing process that requires consistency and effort. Regularly attend events, take part in online communities, and stay in touch with your contacts. Consistent networking efforts can lead to long-term relationships and sustained growth for your business.

Celebrating your networking successes can boost your motivation and morale. Acknowledge and appreciate the connections and opportunities you've gained through networking. Reflecting on your achievements can inspire you to continue building and nurturing valuable relationships.

Chapter 6: Sales Savvy – Close the Deal, Don't Lose the Feel

Mastering the art of selling is crucial for any hustler. This chapter will provide techniques for

closing deals effectively while keeping authenticity and rapport with your clients. Sales is the lifeblood of any business, and this chapter will ensure you're equipped to seal the deal every time.

Understanding your product or service inside and out is the first step to becoming a successful salesperson. Knowing the features  and benefits of unique selling points of what you offer confidence in your product builds trust and credibility with your clients.

Finding your target audience is crucial for effective selling. Understand who your ideal customers are, what their needs and pain points are, and how your product or service can address those needs. Tailor your sales approach to resonate with your target audience and provide relevant solutions.

Building rapport with your clients is essential for setting up trust and credibility. Take the time to get to know your clients, listen actively to their needs, and show genuine interest in their concerns. Building a solid relationship can lead to repeat business and referrals.

Active listening is a crucial skill for successful selling. Pay attention to what your clients say, ask clarifying questions, and show empathy. Understanding your client's needs and concerns allows you to tailor your pitch and provide solutions that meet their needs.

Presenting your product or service effectively involves highlighting the benefits and addressing any objections. Focus on how your product can solve your clients' problems or improve their situation. Use testimonials, case studies, and demonstrations to provide evidence of your product's value.

Handling objections is a crucial part of the sales process. Anticipate common objections and prepare responses that address your client's concerns. Show empathy, provide more information, and reinforce the benefits of your product to overcome objections and move the sale forward.

Creating a sense of urgency can encourage clients to act. Use limited-time offers, exclusive deals, or highlighting the consequences of inaction to motivate clients to decide. However, ensure that your urgency tactics are genuine and not manipulative.

Closing the deal involves confidently asking for the sale. Use closing techniques like the assumptive close, the trial close, or the direct close to guide your clients toward deciding. Be clear and direct in your approach and make it easy for clients to say yes.

Follow-up is crucial for keeping relationships and securing repeat business. After closing a sale, send a thank-you note or follow-up message to express your appreciation. Check-in with your clients regularly to ensure they're satisfied and address any added needs they may have.

Building a referral program can help you generate new leads and expand your customer base. By offering incentives like discounts or rewards, you can encourage satisfied clients to refer their friends and family. A strong referral program can create a steady stream of new business.

Leveraging technology can enhance your sales process. Use CRM tools to manage leads, track interactions, and automate follow-ups. Sales automation tools can streamline your workflow, allowing you to focus on building relationships and closing deals.

Continuous learning is essential for staying ahead in the sales game. Invest in sales training, read books and articles, and attend workshops to improve your skills. Stay updated on industry practices can help refine your sales techniques and achieve better results.

Maintaining a positive attitude is crucial for success in sales. Rejection is a natural part of the process, and a positive mindset can help you stay motivated and resilient. Focus on accomplishments, learn from failures, and keep pushing forward.

Ethical selling involves being honest and transparent with your clients. Avoid making false claims or exaggerating the benefits of your product. Building a reputation for integrity and trustworthiness can lead to long-term success and client loyalty.

Celebrating your sales successes can boost your motivation and morale. Acknowledge and appreciate the deals you've closed and the relationships you've built. Reflecting on your achievements can inspire you to continue honing your sales skills and striving for excellence.

Chapter 7: Balancing the Books – Budgeting for the Hustle

Financial literacy is crucial for sustaining your hustle. This chapter will cover the basics of budgeting, saving, investing, and managing cash flow to ensure your business still is financially healthy and sustainable.

Creating a budget is the first step to managing your finances effectively. A budget outlines your projected income and expenses, helping you plan for the future and make informed financial decisions. Track your income and expenses regularly to ensure you stay within your budget.

Separating your personal and business finances is essential for correct financial management. Open a separate business bank account and use it exclusively for business transactions. This practice simplifies bookkeeping and ensures a clear picture of your business's financial health.

Monitoring your cash flow is crucial for keeping financial stability. Cash flow is the movement of money in and out of your business, and managing it effectively ensures you have enough cash to cover your expenses. Regularly review your cash flow statements and find areas for improvement.

Saving for emergencies is a key aspect of financial planning. Set aside a part of your income in an emergency fund to cover unexpected expenses or downturns in business. An emergency fund provides a financial cushion and helps you navigate challenging times without compromising your business.

Investing in your business can lead to long-term growth and success. Allocate a part of your profits to reinvest in your business, whether for new equipment, marketing campaigns, or employee training. Wise investments can enhance your business's capabilities and competitiveness.

Managing debt is crucial for keeping financial health. Avoid taking on unnecessary debt and prioritize paying off high-interest loans and credit card balances. If you need to borrow, choose financing options with favorable terms and ensure you have a plan to repay the debt.

Understanding your financial statements is essential for making informed decisions. Learn to read and interpret key financial documents like the balance sheet, income statement, and cash flow statement. These statements provide insights into your business's economic performance and health.

Tracking your expenses is crucial for keeping control over your finances. Categorize and check your expenses regularly to find areas where you can cut costs or improve efficiency. Use expense tracking tools or software to streamline this process and ensure accuracy.

Pricing your products or services correctly is vital for profitability. Conduct market research to understand what your competitors charge and what your customers are willing to pay. Set prices that reflect the value you provide while covering your costs and generating a profit.

Tax planning is an essential aspect of financial management. Understand your tax obligations and set aside funds to cover your tax liabilities. Consider working with a tax professional to ensure compliance and take advantage of any tax deductions or credits available to your business.

Financial forecasting helps you plan for the future and make informed decisions. Use historical data and market trends to project your future income and expenses. Regularly update your forecasts to reflect changes in your business environment and adjust your plans accordingly.

Implementing financial controls is crucial for preventing fraud and ensuring accuracy. Establish clear policies and procedures for handling money, and regularly review your financial records for discrepancies. Financial controls help protect your business's assets and support financial integrity.

Outsourcing your bookkeeping and accounting tasks can save time and ensure accuracy. Consider hiring a professional bookkeeper or accountant to handle your financial records, tax filings, and financial reporting. Professional aid can provide peace of mind and allow you to focus on growing your business.

Monitoring vital financial metrics is essential for tracking your progress and making informed decisions. Find metrics that align with your goals, such as gross profit margin, net profit margin, and return on investment. Review these metrics regularly and use the data to guide your financial strategy.

Celebrating your financial milestones can boost your motivation and morale. Acknowledge and acknowledge your progress in managing your finances and achieving your financial goals. Reflecting on your successes can inspire you to continue honing your financial skills and striving for economic stability.

Chapter 8: Juggling Jobs and Jazz Hands

Multitasking and prioritizing tasks are essential skills for any hustler. This chapter will explore techniques for staying organized, avoiding burnout, and keeping a healthy work-life balance while managing multiple responsibilities.

Effective multitasking starts with setting clear priorities. Find the tasks that are most important and urgent and focus on them first. Use to-do lists, priority matrices, and project management software to organize your tasks and ensure you work on what matters most.

Time blocking is a powerful technique for managing your time effectively. Allocate specific blocks of time for different tasks and activities and stick to your schedule as much as possible. Time blocking helps you stay focused, avoid distractions, and minimize.

Delegating tasks can help you manage your workload and free up time for more important responsibilities. Find tasks that others can handle and delegate them to capable team members or outsource them to professionals. Effective delegation allows you to focus on high-impact activities.

Staying organized is crucial for managing multiple responsibilities. Create a system for organizing your tasks, documents, and information. Use digital tools like calendars, task managers, and cloud storage to keep everything in order and easily accessible.

Setting boundaries is essential for keeping a healthy work-life balance. Establish clear boundaries between work and personal life and communicate them to your team and clients. Protect your personal space and make sure to disconnect from work regularly to recharge.

Practicing self-care is crucial for avoiding burnout and keeping your well-being. Make time for relaxing and rejuvenating activities, such as exercise, hobbies, and spending time with loved ones. Prioritizing self-care helps you stay energized and focused on your hustle.

Mindfulness and meditation can help you manage stress and stay present. Incorporate mindfulness practices into your daily routine to improve focus, reduce anxiety, and enhance overall well-being. Taking a few minutes each day to practice mindfulness can have a significant impact. Learning to say no is an essential skill for managing your workload. Understand your limits, and don't take on more than you can handle. Politely decline requests that don't align with your priorities or would stretch you too thin. Saying no allows you to focus on what truly matters.

Setting realistic goals and expectations can help you avoid over-committing. Be honest with yourself about what you can realistically achieve and set achievable goals that align with your priorities. Realistic expectations help you stay motivated and avoid unnecessary stress.

Using productivity techniques like the Pomodoro Technique can enhance your focus and efficiency. Break your work into focused intervals, typically 25 minutes, followed by a short break. This approach helps you stay concentrated, manage time effectively, and prevent burnout.

Regularly reviewing and adjusting your priorities is crucial for staying on track. Periodically  assess your goals and tasks to ensure they align with your aims. Adjust your priorities as needed to reflect changes in your business or personal life.

Building a support system can provide valuable aid and encouragement. Surround

Connect with positive, like-minded individuals who can offer advice, share experiences, and provide support. A strong, robust system can help you navigate challenges and stay motivated.

Balancing multiple responsibilities requires flexibility and adaptability. Be prepared to adjust your plans and priorities as circumstances change. Flexibility allows you to respond effectively to new opportunities and challenges without feeling overwhelmed.

Celebrating small wins can boost your motivation and morale. Acknowledge and appreciate the progress you make, no matter how small. Celebrating your achievements helps you stay positive and motivated on your hustle journey.

Reflecting on your work-life balance regularly can help you make necessary adjustments. Take time to evaluate how well you balance your responsibilities and find areas for improvement. Regular reflection allows you to make intentional changes to enhance your well-being and productivity.

Chapter 9: Creative Crunch Time – Think Outside the Textbook

Innovation and creativity are crucial to standing out in a crowded market. This chapter will explore techniques for encouraging creative problem-solving, embracing innovation, and finding unique solutions to business challenges.

Encouraging creativity starts with creating an environment that  fosters innovation. Create a workspace that inspires creativity, with open spaces, comfortable seating, and plenty of natural light. Encourage brainstorming sessions, idea sharing, and collaboration to stimulate creative thinking.

Embracing a growth mindset can enhance your creativity. View challenges and failures as opportunities for learning and growth. A growth mindset encourages you to take risks, experiment with new ideas, and push beyond your comfort zone.

Diverse perspectives can spark innovation. Surround yourself with a diverse team of individuals with different backgrounds, experiences, and viewpoints. Encourage open discussions and value other opinions to generate various ideas and solutions.

Creative problem-solving involves thinking outside the box. Challenge assumptions, question conventional wisdom, and explore alternative approaches. Use techniques like mind mapping, lateral thinking, and reverse brainstorming to generate new ideas and find unique solutions.

Incorporating play and experimentation into your work can enhance creativity. Set aside time for unstructured exploration, experimentation, and play. Encourage your team to try new things, make mistakes, and learn from their experiences.

Learning from other industries can provide fresh perspectives and ideas. Study businesses and leaders outside your sector to discover innovative approaches and solutions. Adapt and apply these ideas to your business to drive innovation and creativity.

Using design thinking can help you create user-centered solutions. Design thinking is a problem-solving approach that involves empathizing with users, defining their needs, ideating solutions, prototyping, and testing. This iterative process helps you create solutions that meet the needs of your customers.

Collaboration and teamwork can enhance creative problem-solving. Encourage your team to work together, share ideas, and build on each other's insights. Collaborative efforts can lead to more innovative and effective solutions than working in isolation.

Setting aside dedicated time for creativity can boost innovation. Schedule regular "creative crunch time" sessions where you and your team can focus solely on generating ideas and exploring new possibilities. Creating a routine for creativity ensures it stays a priority.

Learning and staying curious is essential for fostering creativity. Continuously seek new knowledge, skills, and experiences to expand your horizons. Attend workshops, read books, take courses, and explore new interests to fuel creativity.

Encouraging risk-taking can lead to innovative breakthroughs. Create a culture where calculated risks are encouraged, and failures are viewed as learning opportunities. Recognize and reward team members who take risks and experiment with new ideas.

Removing barriers to creativity can enhance innovation. Find and cut obstacles that hinder creative thinking, such as rigid processes, excessive bureaucracy, and fear of failure. Create a supportive environment where creativity can flourish.

Seeking feedback and input from customers can provide valuable insights and ideas. Engage with your customers, ask for their opinions, and listen to their needs. Customer feedback can inspire new ideas and help you create solutions that resonate with your audience.

Recognizing and celebrating creative achievements can boost motivation and morale. Acknowledge and reward innovative ideas and solutions, both big and small. Celebrating creativity encourages continued innovation and reinforces its value within your organization.

Reflecting on your creative processes can help you improve and refine them. Review your creative efforts regularly, name what worked well and what didn't, and adjust as needed. Continuous reflection and improvement can enhance your innovative capabilities and drive innovation.

Chapter 10: The Extra Credit – Going Above and Beyond

Going the extra mile can set you apart in the business world. This chapter will emphasize the

importance of exceeding expectations, providing exceptional service, and consistently striving for excellence in everything you do.

Exceeding expectations involves delivering more than what's needed or expected. Look for opportunities to add value and surprise your clients with unexpected benefits. Going above and beyond can create memorable experiences and foster customer loyalty.

Providing exceptional service is crucial for building strong relationships with your clients. Focus on understanding their needs, delivering high-quality solutions, and being responsive and attentive. Outstanding service can differentiate you from competitors and encourage repeat business.

Anticipating your client's needs can help you exceed their expectations. Please consider their preferences and behaviors and proactively offer solutions before they ask. Anticipating needs shows that you understand and care about your client's success.

Personalizing your interactions can enhance your relationships with clients. Use their names, remember details about their preferences, and tailor your communications to their unique needs. Personalization creates a sense of connection and makes clients feel valued.

Addressing issues proactively can prevent them from escalating. Monitor your clients' experiences and address any concerns or issues promptly. Proactive problem-solving proves your commitment to their satisfaction and builds trust.

Continuous improvement is essential for consistently exceeding expectations. Regularly seek feedback from your clients and team and name areas for improvement. Implement changes and innovations to enhance your products, services, and processes.

Investing in your team can enhance your ability to go above and beyond. Provide training, resources, and support to help your  team deliver exceptional service. Empower them to take initiative and make decisions that help your clients.

Creating a culture of excellence within your organization can inspire your team to strive for greatness. Set high standards, recognize and reward outstanding performance, and encourage a mindset of continuous improvement. A culture of excellence fosters a sense of pride and motivation.

Building solid relationships with your clients can lead to long-term success. Take the time to get to know your clients, understand their goals, and build trust. Strong relationships create loyalty and can lead to referrals and repeat business.

Innovating and staying ahead of industry trends can help you exceed expectations. Stay informed about the latest developments in your field and be willing to experiment with new ideas and approaches. Innovation can provide unique solutions and set you apart from competitors.

Providing value beyond your core offerings can enhance your client's experiences. Offer added resources, insights, and support beyond your primary products or services. Providing extra value can strengthen your relationships and create a positive impact.

Maintaining a positive attitude can influence your clients' feelings and experiences. Approach every interaction with enthusiasm, optimism, and a willingness to help. A positive attitude can create a welcoming and enjoyable environment for your clients.

Taking ownership and accountability can build trust and credibility. Own up to mistakes, take responsibility for resolving issues, and follow through on your commitments. Accountability proves integrity and reliability.

Listening to your clients' feedback and acting on it can enhance their satisfaction. Show that you value their opinions by making improvements based on their suggestions. Listening and responding to feedback creates a sense of partnership and shows that you care about their experiences.

Celebrating your successes and acknowledging your efforts can boost motivation and morale. Reflect on the whole that went above and beyond and recognize the positive impact rating your achievements. This reinforces the value of exceeding expectations and inspires you to continue striving for excellence.

Chapter 11: Recess and Recharge – Self-Care for the Hustler

Maintaining your well-being is crucial for sustaining your hustle. This chapter will explore the importance of self-care, stress management, and finding joy and fulfillment in your journey. Taking care of yourself ensures you have the energy and resilience to keep pushing forward.

Self-care is about prioritizing your physical, mental, and emotional well-being. Make time for relaxing and rejuvenating activities, such as exercise, hobbies, and spending time with loved ones. Regular self-care practices help you stay energized and focused on your hustle.

Mindfulness and meditation can help you manage stress and stay present. Incorporate mindfulness practices into your daily routine to improve focus, reduce anxiety, and enhance overall well-being. Taking a few minutes each day to practice mindfulness can have a significant impact. Exercise is crucial for keeping your physical health and energy levels. Find a physical activity you enjoy and make it a regular part of your routine. Exercise improves your physical fitness and boosts your mood and mental clarity.

Getting enough sleep is essential for your overall well-being and productivity. Prioritize a regular sleep schedule and create a relaxing bedtime routine. Quality sleep helps you stay alert, focused, and ready to tackle the challenges of your hustle.

Eating a balanced diet can enhance your energy and focus. Choose nutritious foods that fuel your body and mind and avoid excessive caffeine and sugar. Proper nutrition supports your overall health and well-being.

Taking regular breaks can prevent burnout and keep your productivity. Schedule short breaks throughout your day to rest and recharge. Stepping away from work for a few minutes can help you stay focused and avoid mental fatigue.

Setting boundaries is essential for supporting a healthy work-life balance. Establish explicit boundaries between your work and personal life and communicate them to your team and clients. Protect your individual time and make sure to disconnect from work regularly to recharge.

Finding joy and fulfillment in your hustle can enhance your motivation and well-being. Find what aspects of your work bring you joy and focus on those activities. Pursuing your passions and finding meaning in your hustle can create a sense of purpose and satisfaction.

Building a support system can provide valuable help and encouragement. Surround yourself with positive, like-minded individuals who can offer advice, share experiences, and support. A robust support system can help you navigate challenges and stay motivated.

Practicing gratitude can enhance your

Overall well-being and motivation. Take time each day to reflect on what you're grateful for and acknowledge your achievements, no matter how small. A thankful mindset can shift your focus to your hustle's positive aspects and inspire you.

Learning to say no is essential for managing your workload and avoiding burnout. Understand your limits, and don't take on more than you can handle. Politely decline requests that don't align with your priorities or would stretch you too thin. Saying no allows you to focus on what truly matters.

Engaging in hobbies and activities you enjoy can provide a much-needed break from work. Make time for activities that bring you joy and relaxation, whether reading, painting, gardening, or playing a sport. Hobbies can help you recharge and support a healthy balance.

Spending time with loved ones can provide emotional support and fulfillment. Make time for family and friends and prioritize meaningful connections. Strong relationships and social support can enhance your well-being and resilience.

Reflecting on your self-care practices can help you improve and refine them. Regularly evaluate how well you're taking care of yourself and find areas for improvement. Continuous reflection and adjustment can enhance your self-care routine and overall well-being.

Celebrating your self-care successes can boost your motivation and morale. Acknowledge and appreciate the efforts you've made to prioritize your well-being. Reflecting on your self-care achievements can inspire you to continue caring for yourself and finding joy in your hustle.

Chapter 12: Graduation Day – Celebrate Your Success

Reflecting on your journey and celebrating your achievements is crucial for keeping motivation and recognizing your progress. This chapter will emphasize the importance of acknowledging your successes, planning for future growth, and finding fulfillment in your hustle.

Reflecting on your journey allows you to appreciate how far you've come. Take time to review your goals, milestones, and accomplishments. Reflecting on your progress helps you recognize your growth and the impact of your hard work.

Celebrating your successes can boost your morale and motivation. Acknowledge and appreciate the milestones you've achieved, whether big or small. Celebrating your accomplishments reinforces the value of your efforts and inspires you to keep pushing forward.

Recognizing your strengths and skills can enhance your confidence. Name the skills and qualities that have contributed to your success and find ways to use them in future endeavors. Confidence in your abilities empowers you to take on new challenges and opportunities.

Sharing your achievements with others can create a sense of community and support. Share your success stories with your team, clients, and loved ones. Celebrating together can strengthen your relationships and foster a positive, supportive environment.

Setting new goals is essential for continuous growth and development. Use your reflections on past achievements to set new, ambitious goals for the future. Setting new aims keeps you focused, motivated, and striving for excellence.

Planning for future growth involves finding areas for improvement and opportunities for expansion. Review your business plan, assess your current strategies, and find new growth opportunities. A clear plan for the future helps you stay on track and achieve your long-term goals.

Learning from your experiences is crucial for continuous improvement. Reflect on the challenges you've faced and the lessons you've learned. Use these insights to refine your strategies, avoid past mistakes, and enhance your overall performance.

Finding fulfillment in your hustle involves aligning your work with your passions and values. Reflect on what aspects of your work bring you joy and satisfaction and focus on those activities. Pursuing meaningful work creates a sense of purpose and fulfillment.

Expressing gratitude for the support and opportunities you've received can enhance your relationships and well-being. Take time to thank those who have helped you along your journey, whether it's your team, mentors, clients, or loved ones. Gratitude fosters a positive mindset and strengthens your connections.

Recognizing and rewarding your team can boost their morale and motivation. Acknowledge your team members' contributions and achievements and celebrate their successes. A motivated and appreciated team is likelier to stay committed and perform at its best.

Creating a culture of celebration within your organization can inspire continuous improvement and excellence. Encourage your team to celebrate their achievements, both big and small. A culture of celebration fosters a positive, motivated, and supportive environment.

Reflecting on your impact can provide a sense of fulfillment and purpose. Consider your work's positive impact on your clients, community, and industry. Recognizing the difference, you've made can enhance your sense of accomplishment and motivation.

Relaxing and recharging after significant achievements is essential for keeping your well-being. Celebrate your successes with activities that relax and rejuvenate you, whether a vacation, a spa day, or spending time with loved ones. Rest and relaxation prepare you for future challenges and opportunities.

Continuous investment in personal and professional development is crucial for sustained success. Name areas where you can grow and improve and seek opportunities for learning and development. Continuous investment in yourself enhances your skills, knowledge, and capabilities.

 Celebrating your journey and looking forward to future achievements can inspire you to keep hustling, reflect on your progress, appreciate your successes, and set new goals. Embracing your journey and staying motivated ensures you thrive in your hustle.

Chapter 13: Hustle and Flow – The Rhythm of Success

Maintaining momentum in the long run is essential for sustained  success. This chapter will explore techniques for staying motivated, adapting to changes, and keeping the hustle alive and thriving over time.

Finding your rhythm involves creating routines and habits that support your hustle. Establish a daily schedule that includes time for work, exercise, relaxation, and personal growth. Consistent routines help you stay organized and keep a steady pace.

Staying motivated in the long run requires a clear sense of passion. Find what drives you and keeps you inspired and use it as fuel to support your momentum. Passion and purpose provide the energy and motivation needed to keep pushing forward.

Adapting to changes and challenges is crucial for long-term success. Stay open to new ideas, be willing to pivot when necessary, and embrace change as an opportunity for growth. Flexibility and adaptability help you navigate the ups and downs of your hustle journey.

Continuously setting and revising goals keeps you focused and motivated. Regularly review your goals and progress and set new goals to keep challenging yourself. Setting and achieving goals creates a sense of accomplishment and keeps you moving forward.

Seeking feedback and learning from others can enhance your performance and growth. Engage with mentors, peers, and clients to gather insights and advice. Constructive feedback helps you name areas for improvement and refine your strategies.

Embracing a growth mindset can enhance your resilience and adaptability. View challenges and setbacks as opportunities for learning and development. A growth mindset encourages continuous improvement and helps you stay motivated in adversity.

Balancing work and personal life are crucial for keeping your well-being and productivity. Set boundaries, prioritize self-care, and make time for activities that bring you joy and relaxation. A healthy work-life balance gives you the energy and focus needed for success.

Building a support system can provide valuable aid and encouragement. Surround yourself with positive, like-minded individuals who can offer advice, share experiences, and support. A robust system helps you stay motivated and navigate challenges.

Celebrating small wins can boost your motivation and morale. Acknowledge and appreciate the progress you make, no matter how small. Celebrating your achievements helps you stay positive and motivated on your hustle journey.

Reflecting on your journey and progress can provide valuable insights and motivation. Take time to review your accomplishments, challenges, and lessons learned. Reflection helps you appreciate your growth and stay focused on your long-term goals.

Embracing innovation and creativity can keep your hustle fresh and exciting. Continuously seek new ideas, experiment with new approaches, and stay open to change. Innovation and creativity help you stay ahead in a competitive market and keep enthusiasm.

Managing stress is crucial for supporting your well-being and productivity. Practice mindfulness, meditation, or other relaxation techniques to manage stress and stay focused. Taking regular breaks and allowing yourself time to recharge can prevent burnout and keep you energized.

Building resilience involves developing the ability to bounce back from setbacks. View challenges as learning opportunities and stay persistent in the face of adversity. Resilience allows you to support a positive attitude and keep moving forward, no matter the obstacles.

Continuous learning and development are essential for long-term success. Invest in your education, seek knowledge and skills, and stay curious. Continuous learning enhances your capabilities and keeps you adaptable and competitive.

Finding joy and fulfillment in your hustle can enhance your motivation and well-being. Name what aspects of your work bring you joy and focus on those activities. Pursuing your passions and finding meaning in your hustle creates a sense of purpose and satisfaction.

Chapter 14: Hustle University – Lifelong Learning

Commitment to continuous improvement is crucial for staying ahead in the ever-evolving business world. This chapter will explore the importance of ongoing education, skill development, and staying updated on industry trends and best practices.

Lifelong learning is about continuously seeking new knowledge and skills. Stay curious and open to new ideas and make learning a regular part of your routine. Lifelong learning enhances your capabilities and keeps you adaptable and competitive.

Investing in your education can lead to long-term success. Take courses, attend workshops, and pursue certifications to expand your knowledge and skills. Investing in your education ensures you stay updated on industry trends and best practices.

Reading books and articles can provide valuable insights and inspiration. Make a habit of reading regularly and seek books and articles that align with your interests and goals. Reading broadens your perspective and enhances your understanding of your field.

Seeking out mentors can provide guidance and support on your learning journey. Find mentors with experience and ability in areas you want to develop and build relationships with them. Mentors can offer valuable advice, share their experiences, and help you navigate challenges.

Participating in professional organizations can provide resources and networking opportunities. Join organizations related to your industry and actively take part in their events and activities. Professional organizations offer valuable insights, resources, and connections.

Attending

Conferences and industry events can enhance your knowledge and network. Attend conferences, trade shows, and seminars to learn from experts, stay updated on trends, and connect with like-minded professionals. Industry events provide opportunities for learning and growth.

Online courses and webinars offer flexible and convenient learning opportunities. Explore online platforms that offer courses and webinars on topics relevant to your field. Online learning allows you to access valuable content conveniently and conveniently.

Experimenting and trying new things can enhance your learning and growth. Be willing to step out of your comfort zone, take risks, and experiment with new approaches. Experimentation fosters innovation and helps you discover new opportunities and solutions.

Learning from failures is crucial for continuous improvement. View failures as opportunities for learning and growth and analyze them to find lessons and insights. Learning from failures helps you avoid repeating mistakes and enhances your resilience.

Collaborating with others can enhance your learning and development. Work with colleagues, peers, and experts to share ideas, solve problems, and create new solutions. Collaboration fosters creativity, innovation, and mutual learning.

Staying updated on industry trends and best practices is essential for staying competitive. Regularly research and check developments in your field and adapt your strategies and practices accordingly. Staying updated ensures you stay relevant and informed.

Reflecting on your learning experiences can provide valuable insights and motivation. Please review what you've learned, regularly find key takeaways, and apply them to your work. Reflection helps you combine your learning and recognize your growth.

Embracing a growth mindset can enhance your learning and development. View challenges and setbacks as opportunities for learning and growth. A growth mindset encourages continuous improvement and helps you stay motivated in adversity.

Sharing your knowledge and ability can enhance your learning and reputation. Write articles, give presentations, or mentor others to share your learning. Knowledge reinforces your learning and sets up you as a thought leader in your field.

Celebrating your learning achievements can boost your motivation and morale. Acknowledge and appreciate the progress you've made in your learning journey. Celebrating your achievements reinforces the value of lifelong learning and inspires you to continue seeking new knowledge and skills.

Chapter 15: Epilogue: The Dance Continues

These are my final thoughts and encouragement for embracing the hustle as a lifelong journey. This chapter will cover the importance of the hustle, staying motivated, and continuously striving for excellence in your business and personal life.

Embracing the hustle as a lifelong journey means staying committed to your goals and continuously seeking new opportunities for growth and improvement. Understand that the hustle is not just a phase but a way of life that requires ongoing effort and dedication.

Staying motivated in the long run requires a clear purpose and passion. Name what drives you and keeps you inspired and use it as fuel to keep your momentum. Passion and purpose provide the energy and motivation needed to keep pushing forward.

Reflecting on your journey and progress can provide valuable insights and motivation. Take time to review your accomplishments, challenges, and lessons learned. Reflection helps you appreciate your growth and stay focused on your long-term goals.

Continuously setting and revising goals keeps you focused and motivated. Regularly review your goals and progress and set new aims to keep challenging yourself. Setting and achieving goals creates a sense of accomplishment and keeps you moving forward.

Finding joy and fulfillment in your hustle can enhance your motivation and well-being. Find what aspects of your work bring you joy and focus on those activities. Pursuing your passions and finding meaning in your hustle creates a sense of purpose and satisfaction.

Adapting to changes and challenges is crucial for long-term success. Stay open to new ideas, be willing to pivot when necessary, and embrace change as an opportunity for growth. Flexibility and adaptability help you navigate the ups and downs of your hustle journey.

Building a support system can provide valuable aid and encouragement. Surround yourself with positive, like-minded individuals who can offer advice, share experiences, and support. A robust system helps you stay motivated and navigate challenges.

Celebrating small wins can boost your motivation and morale. Acknowledge and appreciate the progress you make, no matter how small. Celebrating your achievements helps you stay positive and motivated on your hustle journey.

Maintaining a positive attitude can influence your success and well-being. Approach every challenge and opportunity with optimism and enthusiasm. A positive attitude attracts opportunities and inspires those around you, creating a supportive environment for your hustle.

Learning from others and staying curious can enhance your growth and development. Engage with mentors, peers, and experts to gather insights and advice. Continuous learning and curiosity keep you adaptable and competitive.

Taking care of yourself is crucial for sustaining your hustle. Prioritize self-care, manage stress, and keep a healthy work-life balance. Your physical, mental, and emotional well-being ensures you have the energy and resilience to keep pushing forward.

Finding a balance between work and personal life is essential for long-term success. Set boundaries, prioritize self-care, and make time for activities that bring you joy and relaxation. A healthy work-life balance gives you the energy and focus needed for success.

Giving back and helping others can enhance your sense of fulfillment and purpose. Use your skills, knowledge, and resources to support and uplift others. Contributing to your community and positively affecting creates a sense of satisfaction and meaning.

Embracing continuous improvement is crucial for staying ahead in the ever-evolving business world. Regularly seek new knowledge, skills, and experiences to expand your horizons. Continuous improvement ensures you stay competitive and capable of achieving your goals.

The dance of hustle and success is a lifelong journey. Embrace the challenges, celebrate the victories, and stay committed to your goals. The hustle is not just about achieving success but also about enjoying the journey, growing as a person, and positively affecting the world. Keep hustling, and let the dance continue.

Conclusion: Dance Your Way to Success

As we reach the grand finale of our journey, let's put on our dancing shoes and get ready to hustle! Imagine the dance floor of  the business world, where every move you make is a step towards success. Like in the dance, the key to a successful hustle is rhythm, timing, and a bit of flair. So, grab your partner (your who n), and let's dance to the top.

First, let's start with the basics. The hustle begins with a strong foundation, like the basic essential routine. Plant your feet firmly on the ground and remember that every step you take should be with confidence and purpose. Just like in the hustle dance, where you move forward and backward, in business, you must constantly adjust your direction to stay on track.

Now, add a little groove to your steps. In the business hustle, this means bringing in your unique style and personality. Don't be afraid to show off what makes you, well, you! Your individuality is your greatest asset, and it's what will make you stand out in the crowded dance floor of the market.

Next, it's time to spin! Just like those quick twirls on the dance floor, be ready to pivot and adapt. The business world is ever-changing, and the ability to spin on a dime will keep you ahead of the game. When a new opportunity or challenge comes your way, embrace it with a twirl of enthusiasm.

Remember, timing is everything. In the hustle dance, you need to keep up with the beat; in business, it's all about seizing the right moment. Be aware of market trends, listen to your customers, and be ready to act swiftly. Timing your moves correctly can distinguish between a successful deal and a missed opportunity.

As you continue to dance, don't forget the importance of connection. In the hustle, you must stay in sync with your partner. This translates to building strong relationships with your team, clients, and business stakeholders. A synchronized team can move mountains, while a disconnected team can trip over its feet.

Let's not overlook the importance of flair. Every great dancer adds a touch of their own style, and in your hustle, this means going above and beyond. Exceed expectations, surprise your clients with exceptional service, and add a little sparkle that will leave a lasting impression.

While you're grooving to your own beat, make sure to keep an eye on the competition. Like in a dance-off, you must know what your rivals are up to. Study their moves, learn from their successes and mistakes, and use this knowledge to refine your own steps. Staying ahead of the competition means constantly innovating and improving.

Balance is key. In the hustle dance, keeping balance allows you to perform those intricate moves without falling flat. Business is about balancing ambition with  practicality, working with personal life, and risking with reward. Finding this balance will keep you grounded and ensure sustainable success.

And then, there's the footwork. Just like a dancer needs to have precise and swift footwork, in business, you need to be detail-oriented and efficient in business. Paying attention to the finer details and moving with precision can prevent missteps and keep your hustle smooth.

Don't forget the rhythm. Every successful hustle has a rhythm—a consistent, steady pace that drives progress. This rhythm in business comes from setting routines, sticking to your plans, and keeping discipline. A well-maintained rhythm ensures you're always moving forward, even if it's one step at a time.

Now, let's add some pizzazz! Just like in a dance, where a performer might throw in a dazzling move to wow the audience, don't shy away from bold, innovative business ideas in business. Taking calculated risks and daring to be different can set you apart and propel you to new heights.

Engagement is another crucial element. In dance, you need to engage with your audience, and in business, you must engage with your customers. Listen to their feedback, understand their needs, and involve them in your journey. Engaged customers are loyal customers, and they'll keep coming back for more of your dazzling performance.

The hustle is also about endurance. Dancing for hours requires stamina, and so does sustaining a successful business. Keep your energy levels high, care for your health, and keep a positive mindset. Endurance will see you through the long nights and the tough times, keeping you in the game.

Flexibility is your best friend. Just as a dancer needs to be flexible to perform a variety of moves, in business, you need to be flexible in your approach. Be open to new ideas, adaptable to change, and willing to pivot when necessary. Flexibility allows you to navigate the unpredictable twists and turns of the business world.

In the hustle, teamwork makes the dream work. Dancing with a partner requires coordination and cooperation; your team is your greatest asset in business. Foster a collaborative environment, value each team member's contributions, and work together towards common goals. A united team can achieve remarkable things.

Communication is the glue that holds everything together. In dance, non-verbal cues keep partners in sync. Clear and effective communication in business ensures everyone is on the same page. Whether it's with your team, clients, or stakeholders, communicate openly, listen actively, and share your vision.

Let's not forget the importance of practice. Just as a dancer must rehearse tirelessly to perfect their routine, in business, continuous improvement is key. Learn from your experiences, seek feedback, and never stop refining your skills. Practice makes perfect, and dedication to your craft leads to mastery.

The hustle is a dance of resilience. Just as dancers stumble and get back up, in business, setbacks are inevitable in business. The key is to rise each time you fall, learn from your mistakes, and keep pushing forward. Resilience builds strength and character, essential traits for long-term success.

And then there's the grand finale, where you leave a lasting impression. In the business hustle,  this means creating a build a build something that brings you success and success but also makes a positive impact. Your legacy is the ultimate encore, a testament to your journey and contributions.

Celebrate your successes along the way. Just like a dancer takes a bow after a stellar performance, take the time to acknowledge your achievements. Celebrate the milestones, big and small, and appreciate the journey. Recognizing your accomplishments fuels your motivation for the next act.

Surround yourself with inspiration. In dance, watching other great performers can spark new ideas and motivation. In business, seek out mentors, read inspiring stories, and stay connected with those who uplift you. Inspiration keeps your spirit alive and your creativity flowing.

Embrace the spotlight but stay humble. In the hustle, you'll have moments where you're the star show's starry these moments but remember to stay grounded. Humility keeps you connected to your roots and helps you build genuine relationships.

Keep learning new moves. Just as dancers evolve by learning new styles and techniques, continuous learning is vital in business. Stay curious, seek new knowledge, and never stop growing. Adaptability and a willingness to learn keep you ahead of the curve.

Maintain your passion. Dancing is a labor of love, and so is your hustle. Keep your passion alive by doing what you love and loving what you do. Passion is the driving force that makes every step enjoyable and every challenge worth facing.

Remember, every dance has its rhythm, and every hustle has its pace. Find your rhythm, embrace it, and let it guide you, whether it's fast and furious or slow and steady. Your space is your space, and your journey is memorable.

Lastly, enjoy the dance. The hustle isn't just about reaching the destination; it's about savoring every step of the journey. Enjoy the process, relish the challenges, and celebrate the victories. When you dance your way through life with joy and enthusiasm, success is not just an outcome but an ongoing experience.

So, as you step off the dance floor of this book, remember: the hustle is not just a set of moves; it's a way of life. Keep dancing and hustling, and let your

journey be as spectacular as a show-stopping performance. You've got the rhythm, the moves, and the passion—now go out there and dance your way to success!

Check Out A Book Bundle From
Brian's Other Famous Titles
"How To Get Past The Gatekeepers and
Get To Your Goal In Life:
A Personal Guide to Being Persistent"

Bibliography

1. **Covey, Stephen R.** *The 7 Habits of Highly Effective People: Powerful Lessons in Personal Change*. Simon & Schuster, 1989.

2. **Hill, Napoleon.** *Think and Grow Rich*. The Ralston Society, 1937.

3. **Kiyosaki, Robert T.** *Rich Dad Poor Dad: What the Rich Teach Their Kids About Money That the Poor and Middle Class Do Not!*. Plata Publishing, 1997.

4. **Tracy, Brian.** *Goals!: How to Get Everything You Want Faster Than You Ever Thought Possible*. Berrett-Koehler Publishers, 2003.

5. **Sinek, Simon.** *Start with Why: How Great Leaders Inspire Everyone to Take Action*. Portfolio, 2009.

6. **Dweck, Carol S.** *Mindset: The New Psychology of Success*. Ballantine Books, 2006.

7. **Vaynerchuk, Gary.** *Crush It!: Why NOW Is the Time to Cash In on Your Passion*. HarperStudio, 2009.

8. **Cardone, Grant.** *The 10X Rule: The Only Difference Between Success and Failure*. Wiley, 2011.

9. **Ferriss, Timothy.** *The 4-Hour Workweek: Escape 9-5, Live Anywhere, and Join the New Rich*. Crown Publishing Group, 2007.

10. **Thiel, Peter.** *Zero to One: Notes on Startups, or How to Build the Future*. Crown Business, 2014.

11. **Collins, Jim.** *Good to Great: Why Some Companies Make the Leap... and Others Don't*. HarperBusiness, 2001.

12. **Schultz, Howard, and Joanne Gordon.** *Onward: How Starbucks Fought for Its Life without Losing Its Soul*. Rodale Books, 2011.

13. **Maxwell, John C.** *The 21 Irrefutable Laws of Leadership: Follow Them and People Will Follow You*. Thomas Nelson, 1998.

14. **Sincero, Jen.** *You Are a Badass at Making Money: Master the Mindset of Wealth*. Viking, 2017.

15. **Dalio, Ray.** *Principles: Life and Work*. Simon & Schuster, 2017.

NOTES

www.ingramcontent.com/pod-product-compliance
Lightning Source LLC
Chambersburg PA
CBHW071926210526
45479CB00002B/573